LET'S HUG!

EDITED BY
Josleen Wilson

WRITERS
Charles Faraone
Philip Faraone
Paul Planet

DESIGNER
Alis Jordan

PHOTOGRAPHY
J. Gerard Smith

ILLUSTRATION
Alis Jordan

PLANET BOOKS
Bayside, New York

PLANET BOOKS™
Published by
Once Upon A Planet, Inc.
Box 220
Bayside, NY 11361

Printed in the United States of America
Once Upon A Planet is a registered trademark.

First Printing: August 1983

10   9   8   7   6   5   4   3   2   1

Library of Congress Cataloging in Publication Data
Faraone, Charles.
Let's hug!
1. Hugging. I. Wilson, Josleen. II. Faraone, Philip.
III. Planet, Paul. IV. Title.
BF637.H83F37   1983   158'.2   83-11122
ISBN 0-88009-028-6 (pbk.)

Acknowledgments

We'd like to extend our arms in a hug of thanks to all the wonderful huggers everywhere for their encouragement and support; to the hundreds of hug fans who shared their thoughts and feelings; to the radio stations and publications for the invaluable exposure; to the people whose pictures grace the pages of this book; to the creative team at Planet Books who organized the scattered bits and pieces into something beautiful; and to all the fabulous huggers out there who are helping spread the hug message through word of arm.

Contents

hug (hug) *v*. **hugged, hug ging** *v.t*. **1.** to hold closely in one's arms **2.** to keep close to **3.** to squeeze affectionately—*n*. **1.** a close affectionate embrace **2.** a squeeze [From Scandinavian, akin to Old Norse *hugga,* to comfort, console]

Introduction

A few years ago we introduced a line of small, humorous cards and one of them was a *Hug Coupon* (see page 28). The *Hug Coupon* generated so many wonderful letters that we decided to publish a free newsletter for hug lovers. The newsletter attracted a lot of publicity and a flood of new letters followed. From there we produced a little book about hugging, and still more letters arrived. We finally decided to take all the great ideas, letters, photographs, experiences, and feelings we'd accumulated and create a very special book with a simple aim: Get more people to do more hugging. We've done our part—now we'll leave it all up to you. There's a hugging revolution going on and we're proud to be a part of it. We hope *Let's Hug!* convinces you to take matters into your own arms and add more hugging to our world. Two-gether we can make a difference.

Chapter One

My Best Hug

The Hug
I Love

There's a hug to say
I love you
and a hug to say goodbye
there's a hug to say
how are you?
and a hug to say we tried
there's a hug to bond
a friendship
and a hug when the
day is through
but the hug that's best
in all the world
is the hug I share
with you.

MAILBAG

I come from a hugging family of twelve children. My father and brothers hugged bear hugs, hugs so big they lifted you off the floor. My mother's hugs were warm and enveloping; she had the softest bosom and she always wore Radio Girl cologne, which was a very popular fragrance in the 1930s. I don't know which hugs were "the best," but when I went home after my Dad passed away, my mother held me in her arms and hugged me, and her wonderful perfume reminded me of the closeness we all shared and always would.

J.D.G.
Alameda, California

"...somehow that hug gave me fresh hope."

Many years ago when I left home I stopped by the parish house to say goodbye to my priest. I was about seventeen, and I had known this man most of my life, and up until then life hadn't been so hot. My priest had helped me through some tough spots, but he was a very reserved person, and our relationship had always been rather formal. Somehow I felt disturbed saying goodbye to him. And when he stood on the church steps and held out his arms to me I started to cry. I hugged him so hard; somehow that hug gave me fresh hope. Twenty-five years later I can still remember exactly how it felt.

J.M.D.
Chicago, Illinois

When I lay desperately ill in the coronary care unit at the hospital a young seminary intern from our church came to visit. He barely knew me but as soon as he walked into my room, he put his arms around me and held me. It was the first hug I had received in as long as I could remember. No one can ever know how much it meant to me—I feel perhaps that hug was the difference between life and death.

Dr. Marilyn L. Pinheiro
Toledo, Ohio

Maybe a week after meeting my Joanna we spent the evening talking and drinking endless cups of tea. When I finally said goodnight I reached out to her and gave her a hug—not a kiss, not a pass, just a hug.

From that night on our relationship developed and six months later we were married. Now, 25-plus years later I believe that hug will always be with me.

Lawrence Rosano
Placerville, California

My grandma's hugs are the best. I feel sorry for anyone who doesn't have a grandma to hug them at least 100 times a day.

Jill, age 6
New York, New York

There's no doubt about it. My best hug was the first time I hugged my newborn daughter, Anna. I'll never forget it.

Mary Libraro
Jamaica Estates, New York

Hugs That Comfort

There comes a time when we all want to sit back and get loved. And there's no better way than with the fine, easy comfort of hugging.

Inspired by the human condition, this world-famous method of communication is wonderful straight, or mixed with any style of behavior.

Hugging is one of the best comforts of life.

Hugging Is Practically Perfect:

- No movable parts
- No batteries to wear out
- No periodic checkups
- Low energy consumption
- High energy yield
- Inflation-proof
- Nonfattening
- No monthly payments
- No insurance requirements
- Theft-proof
- Nontaxable
- Nonpolluting
- And, of course, fully returnable

Some of the Best Things Are Measured by the Squeeze

HUGGING

The symbol of luxury. Enjoy quality in excess.

Hugs Are Free

Maybe that's why so many people take them for granted. If hugs did cost a lot of money, people would probably knock themselves out to make money to buy hugs.

Even though hugs are free, hugs aren't worth anything if they aren't used. And a hug not used is lost forever. On an affection-starved planet, can we really afford to waste hugs?   ♥

Chapter Two

Getting Hugs Started

Caution... Advice to Beginners

Never hug a porcupine
or try to squeeze a snake,
Though hugging's good for
most of us
use care, for safety's sake.

The bull, the shark, the elephant
are dangerous hugs for sure,
A cuddle could have side effects
for which there is no cure.

Who you should or should not hug
is often hard to tell,
Why, if you tried to hug a skunk
you might not like the smell.

But when it comes to human beings
just put your fears to rest,
You'll find most arms are open to
a simple hug request.

♥

MAILBAG

I received a *Hug Coupon* from a friend about a year ago, and was so touched by its effect on me that I, in turn, mailed it to a friend who was a patient in a neuropsychiatric hospital. Needless to say, he was overjoyed because he needed that extra, caring stroke.

I am a registered nurse, and my professional life has often led me through the valley of aging and dying patients. I feel that our human future depends on caring and increased value ethics. That's why the *Hug Coupon* has meant so much to me.

Joan Sylvia
Waynesboro, Virginia

"...I think I've started an epidemic."

I teach parapsychology and self-development classes. Some of my students haven't been hugged in years. And many have never experienced affection without demand. When I initiate hugging at the end of class there are always a few gasps, giggles, and groans but it doesn't take long for the teeming masses to merge. "Clump hugging" has even become quite popular. Step two is a little harder—hug yourself at least once a day while saying "I love you." You've probably guessed step three—an "I love you" happens naturally when hugging someone else.

My students respond quickly to this acceptance and caring and become openly caring themselves. They begin to accept themselves for whatever they are or are not.

Bridget T. Webb, R.N.
North Tonawanda, New York

In a family I know, the man of the house does not hug. His wife and daughter gave him *Hug Coupons*, along with hugs, which he accepted, but to which he did not respond. Then they told him they needed some coupons back because he had them all. It was a good way to coax him out of his passive role, and encourage him to be an active hugger.

Laura Newman
Gainesville, Florida

I'm the oldest freshman in my college class (age 21, my last birthday). When I arrived early on campus for orientation I didn't fit in very well. So I handed out a few note cards advertising that "I give hugs...any time of day or night... I am open armed." Since then, many people have come to me for hugs, and I think I've started an epidemic. Now I'm known as "The Hugger" or "Huggles."

Michael Hoffman
Duluth, Minnesota

Yesterday my partner and I met with a business associate who is always standoffish. She's a wonderful human being, but she has a tough exterior and you could talk all day trying to get her to agree to a hug. Like a lot of people, she'd tell you it was silly, unnecessary, ridiculous, a waste of time, and the like.

Sometimes you just can't give people a chance to say no. So, yesterday one of us threw his arms around her and, of course, she protested, but she wasn't let loose. After about 30 seconds, she said, "Wow, a person could get to like that," and when the hug ended she immediately initiated another one. Suddenly, she was a different person, saying how great it felt and all, and when the second hug ended, she practically demanded a hug from the other one of us, and of course she got it.

Sometimes I think you have to take up arms and attack—but you have to do it with love and you have to make sure you're not threatening about it. Everyone needs and wants hugging.

Ray Presti
New York, New York

> ## "Sometimes I think you have to take up arms and attack..."

♥

LET THE MAGIC TOUCH YOU

There's magic in the air, and you'll find it in hugging. What a show! A unique entertainment...and no one else in the world can imitate your hug. Let the magic touch you. You'll find it bewitching.

Recipe For A Perfect Hug

Hug Recipe

Ingredients:

- 2 people
- 4 arms
- 2 hearts
- A touch of love
- A pinch of humor
- A sprinkle of glee

Directions:

Extend arms and wrap them around each other. Clear your minds, take a good look at each other, then pull yourselves together and mix well.

Serves two.

The Hug Kit

Directions:

1. Cut coupon and button cover along dotted lines.
2. Take button cover and paste over any ordinary button.
3. Wear button.
4. Present coupon to HUGGEE.
5. Hope for the best.

I'm a Participating Human Being

HUG COUPON

FREE

"Good for one hug, redeemable from any participating human being."

©ONCE UPON A PLANET Box 220 Bayside, N.Y. 11361 PC41

HUG COUPON

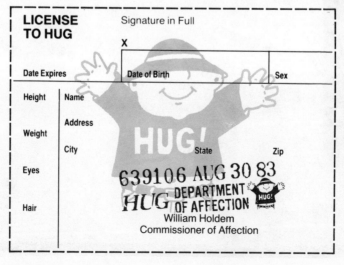

LICENSE TO HUG

Signature in Full

X

| Date Expires | Date of Birth | Sex |

Height	Name
Weight	Address
	City	State	Zip
Eyes	
Hair	

639106 AUG 30 83

HUG DEPARTMENT OF AFFECTION

William Holdem
Commissioner of Affection

You Can Do It!

The frustration I feel
knowing things could be different
if only I could open my heart
if only I would open my arms
makes me wonder why I can't
makes me wonder why I won't.

Come Out Of The Closet

The Time Has Come
To Take Up Arms.

Mini Poster

PHOTOCOPY AND CUT ALONG DOTTED LINE

Chapter Three

Passing It On

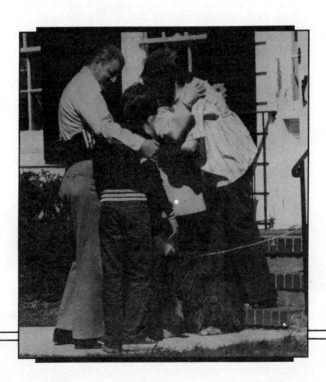

The Best People, Places And Times To Hug:

- Anyone
- Anyplace
- Anytime

MAILBAG

When I went to college it was the first time I had ever been away from home. I missed my folks, and especially my little sisters. After Christmas break I initiated hug therapy at school. I knew I couldn't be the only student who was homesick. I thought hugs could cheer and brighten all our days. People began knowing me for my hugs and my hug collection of writings and studies. This year I am a faithful hug therapist, open to hug anyone, to assure that they, and I, get at least four hugs a day. My favorite door sign to tell people where I am is one that reads, "HUG HUNTING." Hugs have made my life so happy, and it's great to share hugs with everyone! Don't let anyone go unhugged today.

Laura Bender
Oswego, New York

"Don't let anyone go unhugged..."

Hugs are kind of like smiles. They aren't worth anything until you give or receive one, but once you do, their worth is immeasurable. Don't keep hugs to yourself. Give one to somebody else, or ask somebody to give you one. They're free for the asking!

M.E.D.
Elmont, New York

My sister and I mail *Hug Coupons* out in Christmas cards and birthday cards, and give them to friends for no reason at all, except that we want them to have them. We are trying to do our part in spreading the hug crusade.

M.B.
Seattle, Washington

In the summer of 1982 I joined the Great Alaska Bike Trek—a 4,400-mile odyssey from Anchorage, Alaska, to Long Beach, California, to promote and raise funds for the Mental Health Association. We were 27 volunteers, ranging in age from 15 to 70. Together we became a family on an incredible journey.

At the first group meeting I expressed a desire for more affection among the members. At the next meeting our leader invited everyone to join the hug club. I was so high from hugs that night that when I came across a neighboring camper, I threw my arms around him without thinking and gave him quite a start! A few weeks and many miles later, we met again in another campground and he remembered me and the hug.

The hug club was an integral part of the trek, along with variations such as mass (and dangerous!) group hugs, hug tolls, very quick hugs (during the weeks between showers) and my personal favorite, hypothermia hugs. People began to know when someone needed a hug for support, comfort, encouragement, or just to say, "I like you."

Those sincere hugs made all the long hours in the saddle, cold weather, torrential rains, Alaskan mosquitoes, hills, media, city smog and traffic more tolerable.

"Hugs are kind of like smiles."

After 80 days on the road we rolled into Long Beach on August 30, ecstatic with the thrill of victory, humble and thankful that we were still 27 strong. And there in the crowd was a woman searching frantically for the girl who hugged her son on a campground in Alaska! Ah, the power of hugs.

I'd like to say thank you to all the members of the GABT for all the hugs that made that summer so special.

Nancy Baker
Torrance, California

When I was in high school I started a "Hug Day," which later became a tradition. The 13th of each and every month was a hug day (except in February, when we extended it to the 14th, Valentine's Day). So even kids can pass it on. Get out the hug.

Kimberly J. Libby
Columbus, Ohio

I've been a hug advocate for as long as I can remember. I consider myself something of a "hugspert." Now, with cards and booklets I have even more ways to share hugs with distant friends. A hug in the mail can bring instant smiles and warmth, like all hugs do. I know, because I received one when I was having a bad day and it made the whole day better. Wishing you many open arms, and peace.

Lisa Purcell
Lewistown, Pennsylvania

The best part about hugging is—you don't have to wait to get one to go around giving hugs. I love it! Hugs to you and yours.

K.T.
New York State

If you see a friend who looks down or lonely or bummed out or just plain not right, help her/him out by asking if she/he "needs a hug." It may be the perfect remedy to whatever is not good. And, if not, at least the person knows you care about her/his emotional welfare.

Amos
Worcester, Massachusetts

Wherever I go I find people to hug and tell them to pass it on. Most people are taken aback at first, but end up smiling and agreeing to pass it on.

Marianne Losardo
Lackawanna, New York

♥

"I NEVER KNEW HUGS FELT LIKE THIS."

Try a hug—the smooth alternative to shaking hands. The first touch will amaze you. The second will convert you.

Make sure it's a hug from someone you like. Hugs have been shared by human beings since the beginning of time. Your own special dedication will produce hugs of exceptional purity and quality. No wonder the best hugs in this country come from people with open arms.

The
HUG ARM-Y
WANTS YOU!

If you have two arms and you would like to make this planet safe for HUGOCRACY, contact your local recruiter. Now is your chance to serve your planet as you serve yourself.

☆ ☆ ☆

The all-new HUG ARM-Y can use a few good arms.

Desk Signs

PHOTOCOPY AND CUT ALONG DOTTED LINE

PLEASE
SQUEEZE
THE
HUMAN

FOLD HERE

I
L♥VE
HUGGING

© ONCE UPON A PLANET Box 220 Bayside NY 11361

Hug Hit List

Start a list of people to hug, and don't let yourself cop out. Unless you are radically different from most people you'll probably put off making a move and then forget what you wanted to do. Date your list so you'll know just how long your procrastination is taking. Re-member, everyone loves hugging (even people who say they don't), but the well has to be primed, and that's where you come in. If you're wishing for someone else to start the ball rolling, stop wishing and start hugging among family and friends. What do you say?

People to Hug   Date

_____   _____

_____   _____

_____   _____

_____   _____

_____   _____

_____   _____

_____   _____

_____   _____

_____   _____

_____   _____

_____   _____

"Never put off for tomorrow what can be communicated today, because tomorrow might be too late."   **PAUL PLANET**

Mini Poster

PHOTOCOPY AND CUT ALONG DOTTED LINE

GONE HUGGING

WILL BE BACK AT:

Chapter Four

Who Needs Hugs?

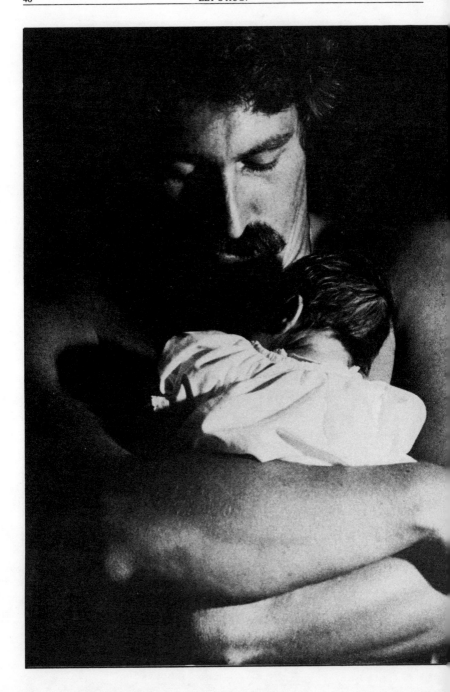

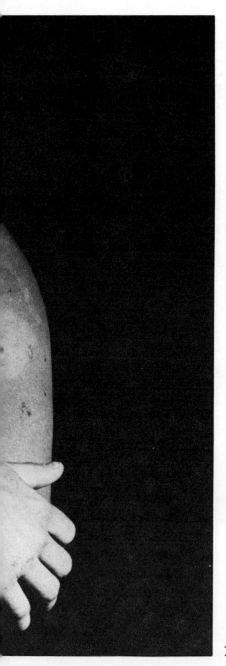

Adults, Infants and Hugging

Adults love to hug babies and they do it as often as possible. Adults love to hug other adults too, yet they seldom do. The reason for this inconsistency is surprisingly simple. Adults are not afraid to initiate and enjoy hugging with infants because there's little chance of rejection.

MAILBAG

I'm on a coed football team at school and tonight we played an important playoff. All through the game, whenever the other players made a play, a tackle, or just tried their best, I hugged them or gave them a pat on the back. We won! But the best part of the game was not the winning; it was the joy I felt hugging my teammates. I have a hard time showing my feelings to other people, and tonight I did it so freely and naturally that it felt wonderful. Maybe I'll try it more often.

Joy Michele Bornstein
Beachwood, Ohio

"I have become so addicted to hugging..."

I have a kitty named Sam that I like to hug, and so does everybody in my family because when you hug him he purrrrrrrrrs. Sam likes hugs a lot and I think he would hug me back if he could.

Rosie, age 9
Cleveland, Ohio

A warm fuzzy is a glow you feel inside, usually while or after something nice has happened. A letter from a friend can produce a warm fuzzy; so can a compliment, or a smile. Hugs are definitely warm fuzzies. The opposite of a warm fuzzy is a cold prickly, but we don't discuss *those*.

Amy J. Bromberg
Edison, N.J.

I first encountered the happy, healthy hug in Alcoholics Anonymous, where "warm fuzzies" are a way of life. There's no doubt in my mind that hugging helps, and I have tried to hug where no man has hugged before. But sometimes the walls are too tough. Maybe if I build up my hug reservoir I will be able to hug the presently un-huggable in the future. Where there's a hug, there's hope.

Chris C.
Scituate, Massachusetts

One of the first things I tell our new nursing aides is that touching and hugging are the most important things they can do to help our nursing-home residents live full lives.

Our volunteers sometimes hold people in their arms who can barely stand to "dance"—really only swaying to music. Volunteers and aides learn that a hug or kiss from them can mean the difference between a really blah day and a really special day. Personally, I have become so addicted to hugging that I can hardly contain myself. Having been both huggee and hugger, I know that nothing else, even medication, works quite so well.

Jane Lou Smith
Pottstown, Pennsylvania

I am a 66-year-old brother who taught English and Latin for 39 years. Now, in retirement, I act as a part-time chaplain to a local hospital and nursing home. I make sure to hug the old people in the nursing home—it does us all a lot of good. Sincerely in hugdom.

Br. Dennis Flynn
Leonardtown, Maryland

I'm living in a building for retired senior citizens, and if anyone needs a hug often it's us. Especially me, since I have no family to hug or hug me. I am 76 years of age, and as of today I shall bestow my hugs upon a few close and dear friends that I have made since coming to my new home, three years ago.

Evelyn G. (Billie) Shriver
Takoma Park, Maryland

"I make sure to hug the old people..."

My name is "HUGGS" the Clown. I got my name several years ago when our church congregation began shaking hands as a sign of peace. Shaking hands is great if you're a businessman, but not for me. I began to hug people in church. When I later became a clown I could hug everybody, especially at nursing homes and hospitals. Sometimes I find hugs are better than any words. I know my performances are a success when everyone waits in line for a big hug.

I also teach 7th grade. When a child misbehaves I know that what he or she really wants is attention. In my class any misdemeanor is greeted with a big hug in front of the whole class. Although I have the best behaved class in school, the kids often come back after class or drop by my home for a private little hug. I give out *Hug Coupons* as special rewards, and hand them out to people as I walk around hospitals, especially to those who are shy.

HUGGS (Joan E. Brugnone)
Alsip, Illinois

WHAT SORT OF PEOPLE NEED HUGGING?

Nice people • People who like to share nice things • People who make themselves and the world they live in a little bit happier through hugging • People like you.

We All Need Hugs

Butchers, bakers, candlestick makers, acrobats, clowns, cheerleaders, joggers, magicians, musicians, singers, dancers, drivers, runners, walkers, crawlers, hobos, farmers, engineers, husbands, wives, daddies, mommies, daughters, sons, brothers, sisters, grandmas, grandpas, aunts, uncles, cousins, friends, enemies, teachers, ministers, rabbis, priests, nuns, nurses, doctors, tailors, bartenders, writers, judges, babysitters, city folk, country folk, bosses, secretaries, assistants, receptionists, soldiers, sailors, waitresses, waiters, movie stars, mechanics, orphans, gardeners, accountants, lawyers, pilots, artists, programmers, politicians, queens, kings, princesses, princes, students, plumbers, electricians, carpenters, jewelers, lifeguards, ball players, coaches, announcers, in-laws, agents, dentists, models, designers, architects, photographers, printers, machinists, welders, cooks, dishwashers, painters, comedians, boys, girls, women, men, principals, teenagers, janitors, retailers, wholesalers, bookkeepers, tellers, guards, disc jockeys, jockeys, sales people, fire people, police people, mail people, weather people, repair people, happy people, lonely people, shy people, tall people, skinny people, heavy people, sick people, healthy people, old people, young people, princely people,

simply, people.

Chapter ♥ Five

It Takes All Kinds

Styles of Hugs

Some believe that trying to define hugs is like trying to define the universe. Others feel more comfortable with names and labels. Still others feel it doesn't matter what you call a hug, as long as you feel it. "How" you hug isn't nearly as important as "that" you hug. Stick to the classic bear hug or experiment with the examples of creative hugging on the following pages. The only limits are in your mind.

BUNNY HUG

HAND HUG

SEEDY HUG

BACK ATTACK HUG

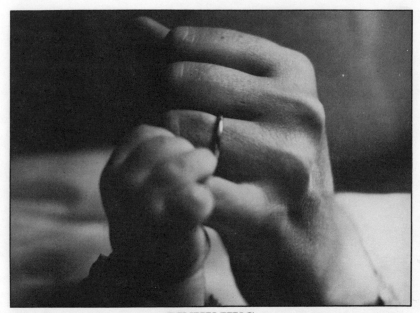

PINKY HUG

BELLY HUG

HEAD HUG

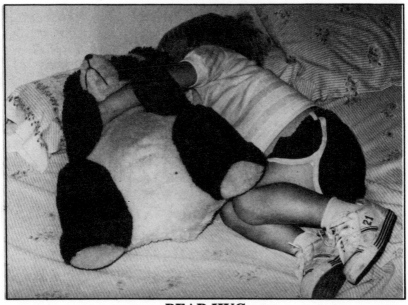

BEAR HUG

MAILBAG

Our church is full of "Huga-bodies." It can really change life. When we can't see each other in person we call each other up and say "mmmm-mmmm." That's a hug over the phone. It also works in a letter. So "mmmm-mmmm" to you all.

Janet Easterwood
Tomball, Texas

When all else fails—the self-hug ain't bad. Although a person with long arms would do better.

Tom
Long Island, New York

Even though I'm only a high school youngster, I fully appreciate a simple expression of affection.

Hugging is spreading rapidly among my circle of friends as the most popular form of greeting. (Who cares whether we're holding stacks of books?) I think it illustrates that today's youth needs affection and love, too. When the pressures brought on by fear-of-peer - condemnation - over - touching - someone - other - than - one's- "steady" are overcome in order to receive some genuine human kindness (breath!), either the social taboos are being broken down, or we're expressing a dire need. Or a little of both.

"...square dancers love to hug."

The hug gospel is being preached all over America, and a new revolution is coming! Much love and many hugs.

Peggy Robyn Wright
Fairfax Station, Virginia

I'm an incarcerated inmate who's into hugging. I landed here because I was raised to keep my mouth shut, just one of those things. I know you didn't ask me, but I just want to tell someone I'm not a bad person because I'm here. I'm not a bad person and it's not my nature to hurt or take things that aren't mine. I want someone to know.

A friend

A hug out of context is a hug lost. Both parties have to know that a hug is imminent. Outstretched arms is the most obvious signal. For some reason, the image I first get in my mind of a hug is two Russians on a snowy street in Moscow with big brown fur coats and bulky hats rushing up to one another and embracing in an enormous hug. This is indeed a happy moment. Even behind the Iron Curtain—a hug is a hug.

Tom Stock
Smithtown, New York

Just like everyone else, square dancers love to hug. We have a special call for hugging that always brings an enthusiastic response, even at the least expected time: "YELLOW ROCK!"

Jack E. Richman
Oakdale, Minnesota

"I'm an incarcerated inmate who's into hugging."

I love all us huggers going out and opening our arms just one more time. I'm in a personal growth training seminar where there's a lot of hugging. We even demonstrate different hugs, and we've got a wide variety.

But the ultimate is the "full-chakra" hug, when all the chakra centers are aligned allowing greater flowing of the loving presence, and the merging of the one heart. God's peace.

Frank James Cardamone
Woodstock Valley, Connecticut

♥

The Hug-Word Puzzle

ACROSS

1. A great way to greet friends
2. Never _____ an octopus
3. Even a child can do it
5. Rhymes with TUG
6. Everyone can use a _____
8. Instead of fighting
10. For comfort
11. Embrace

DOWN

1. Never turn down a _____
2. What to do when words won't do
3. Instead of eating
4. To stay healthy
6. When you're scared
7. The _____ Arm-y wants you!
8. What this book is trying to get you to do
9. Let's _____

Chapter Six

Sex And
The Single Hug

Two Different Things

Hugging feels so good that a lot of people confuse hugging with sex, and that's really too bad. This unfortunate misunderstanding causes people who are afraid of sex to avoid hugging. It leads others to sexual promiscuity when all they really want is to be hugged.

Sex and hugging are two different things. A hug is a hug is a hug and people must stop thinking about hugging as a means to an end. Hugging is a wonderful, beautiful, loving end all by itself.

♥

MAILBAG

In my country, Brazil, many people hug and I've observed that we really get closer to other people. It is not easy, though, because the first step must be "hugging through the mind." It is not worth a body hugging without a mind hugging! (I hope you understand my English.)

Eduardo
Brazil

It's good to see that in a world where all the emphasis appears to be on sex, some people recognize that more affection can be put into one good hug than in a whole evening of sex (and without compromising one's virginity).

D.S.B.
New York State

Warm, friendly hugs are *not* sexual. Some people have a difficult time dealing with this, for any physical contact is interpreted as sexual by those who do not recognize the heart's need for cuddling. Hugs are definitely part of sexual intimacies, but taken in friendship with warm intentions, hugging is beautifully sensual, not sexual.

Amy J. Bromberg
Edison, N.J.

It's about time this country had something like hugs, and I hope it spreads to the U.N. Wouldn't that be great! Now all we need is for every school to teach a course in hugging survival.

I agree about hugging being mistaken for sexual interest. I used to feel that way, then I saw hugging for what it really is, and a light came on at the end of a long, dark tunnel. Hugs forever.

Sue Downes
Royal Oak, Michigan

"Warm, friendly hugs are not sexual."

Hugging little girls and older women is OK, but there's no substitute for hugging girls your own age who are not relatives (I am 28 and single). No matter how many hugs you have from other people, something important is missing when you don't get or give hugs to the opposite sex of your own age. In fact, I think it's the most important hugging of all. Well, that's my belief anyway. How does anyone else feel about this?

Jack Giammerse, Jr.
Baton Rouge, Louisiana

How does one get started? It's easy to say, "Just go up to someone and hug them." But it's not that easy to put into practice, especially when you're not a demonstrative person by nature, and neither is anyone else around you. Plus, you have to work mostly with members of the opposite sex who regard a hug either as a come-on or a threat of some kind. Can anyone share his or her feelings about this? Help!

D.C. Culbertson
Baltimore, Maryland

♥

HAVE YOU SHARED YOUR HUGS WITH HIM YET?

It's an idea whose time has come. For millennia women all over the world have made hugging part of a tradition of friendship. But lately, men have discovered hugging's unique quality. To their great pleasure. So consider sharing your hugs with him tonight.

HUGGING

The All-New **HUGDLE** Is Here

That's right, after years of research and testing it's here and available to you. Not just another hug; more than a cuddle, the HUGDLE is a new dimension in affection. Give it a try and discover why men and women the world over are saying, "It's undoubtedly the greatest thing since touching!"

Unconditional Guarantee

If for any reason you are not completely satisified with your HUGDLE, just return it to your authorized representative and you will receive a replacement free of charge.

The French Have A Name For It...
Embrasser

HINT #1 FROM PAUL PLANET

How To Improve Your Social Life:

If you're leaving singles bars still single, if you're getting nothing but healthy at the local health club—take heart.

With the magic of hugging, you'll have great opening lines to help you make new friends. Lines like, "Hi, how are you?"

Sound trite? Not when accompanied by a warm hug. Hugs can satisfy even the most demanding people—from society matrons to movie stars. Hugging is so easy even a not-so-smooth operator can succeed. Hugs come with a built-in variety to put real magic in your social life.

If you need a break from all your newfound popularity, you'll have to tie your arms to your sides. But in the meanwhile open up and see just how much magic you can bring into your life.

Hugging...Bring The Magic Home

Chapter Seven

Ask Doc Hug

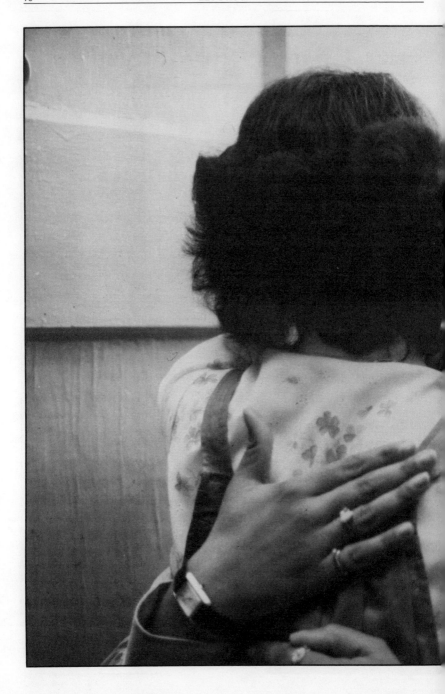

Hugging Is Healthy

- It helps the body's immune system
- It keeps you healthier
- It cures depression
- It reduces stress
- It induces sleep
- It's invigorating
- It's rejuvenating
- It has no unpleasant side effects
- Hugging is nothing less than a miracle drug

MAILBAG

I like *Hug Coupons* so much that I bought them for several friends. I even gave them to my therapist. He (and the clinic he works in) really gets into hugging. He's like hugging a live, warm, fuzzy teddy bear! He taught me how to give and receive hugs, so I gave him a teddy bear for him and other clients to hug, and it's been a huge success. Warm fuzzies.

Sue

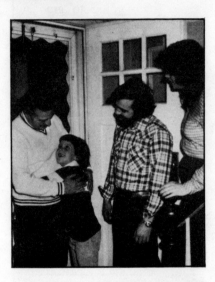

"…I kiss and hug my older friends every chance I get."

I work with the elderly in my community, and do a lot of hugging. The seniors like to hug. Whenever I speak to a group I ask them have they had at least three hugs a day? I set the pace because I kiss and hug my older friends every chance I get.

Dee Magnani
Tucson, Arizona

About a year ago I had to give up a position at the top of my profession because of increasing disability. Since then I have been through a very difficult period of trying to adjust to my physical limitations. Being alone has become hard to bear at times. A pamphlet I read recommends three hugs per day for diabetics. I'm not a diabetic but I know I would feel so much better if a "hug prescription" could be carried out in my case. I think everyone, especially those who are alone, ill, or old, could use as many hugs as they can be given.

Dr. Marilyn L. Pinheiro
Toledo, Ohio

I am a psychotherapist in private practice. My practice began with my completing my own therapy then going to graduate school in social work. The type of therapy I offer is called Parenting/Reparenting. I work in a group private practice with my mother and sister. We hug and touch each other, our clients, our friends, and all others. Part of the program we teach supports clients who are

"…at least three hugs a day."

lonely, frightened, isolated or lacking in social contacts to hug, do spoons with others, trade backrubs, and generally to learn to be a warm, affectionate person. All this in a nonsexual way. Many people at first think that touching is only sexual and have trouble accepting or giving strokes. Many don't have permission to be openly affectionate. (By the way, spoons is an activity where people lie down together in succession with a back to a front to a back and so on. It looks like a row of spoons all snuggled together.) I recommend touching to everyone. I am very gratified in my work to see and be

a part of people's change from scared, lonely, froglike existences to living like they were meant to—aware, satisfied and competent individuals.

Ryan Elliott
Chicago, Illinois

I have been an extoller of the benefits of "hugtherapy" for most of my 38 years. I have perfected the "rolling hug" and will demonstrate it at any opportunity. Hugtherapy has also proven absolutely mind-boggling in the field of migraine cures.

Patricia Donovan
New York, New York

It's really good to know that some people still care about feeling good inside and hugging can help you do that.

Shannon Congdon (age 12)
Sharon Knight (age 13)
Quincy, Florida

♥

Hugging Is All Natural

- Organic
- Naturally sweet
- No pesticides
- No preservatives
- No artificial ingredients
- 100% wholesome

"Experts will tell you they approve of hugging because of its therapeutic nature, meditative effect and pleasant reaction. What they mean is…it feels good."

The Pleasure Is Back

HUGGING

Doc Hug's Favorite Questions

Q. When my friends meet they say, "Slap me five." Does hugging have a greeting like that?

A. "Wrap me two!"

Q. Is there really a minimum daily requirement for hugs?

A. Yes. As many hugs as you can get from oodles of people, give or take a hug.

Q. Is there anything better than hugging?

A. Not that I know of—but anything's possible.

Q. Did you ever get the feeling that hugging is too good to be true?

A. All the time. It's my favorite feeling.

Q. With all it has going for it, why isn't hugging running amuck?

A. Fear, ignorance, fear, macho, fear, silliness, b.o., and fear.

Q. Sometimes when I hug my husband it feels like we're dissolving into each other. Is there any advice you can give us about this wonderful "free" form of travel?

A. Go with the flow!

Q. Does any one group of people require more hugging than any other?

A. Not enough to matter. When in doubt, hug!

Q. What are some of your favorite songs to hug to?

A. "What the World Needs Now" and "Heaven, I'm in Heaven."

Q. How many calories do you burn off during a good hug?

A. Very few, but they add up.

Q. Is hugging addictive?

A. You bet!

Q. I really want to hug my friend and I know he wants to hug me. Yet we still can't seem to get things started. Why?

A. You're thinking too hard about it; do it!

Q. Is it possible to like hugging too much?

A. Noooooooooo way!

Doc Hug

Hours: _____ By Appointment

Name _*You*_ _____ Date _*Today*_

As many
HUGS as
you can get

Repeat _*Daily*_ _____

Chapter Eight

When You Need It Bad...

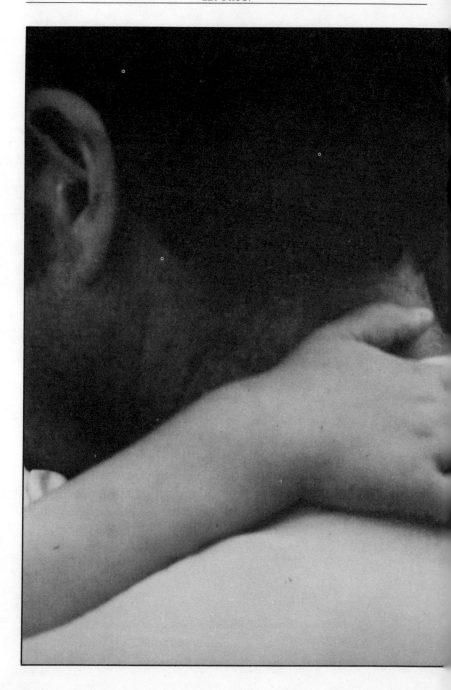

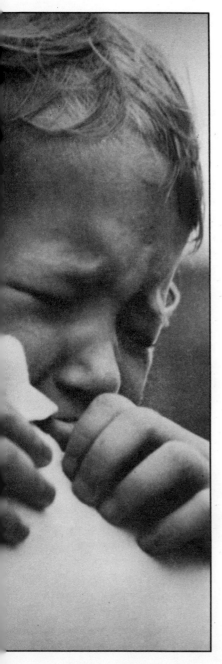

The Essentials Of Life

1. Air
2. Food
3. Water
4. Love
5. **Hugging**
6. Clothing
7. Shelter

♥

MAILBAG

At our counseling center we have an ongoing growth group. One of the members came in one evening and announced that she was deprived: "It takes four hugs a day to survive, and I haven't even had the minimum, so I need some hugs!" After that, we began exchanging hugs every time we met—each person in the group with everyone else. We've all become expert huggers. Warmest.

Laura Newman
Gainesville, Florida

"What a wonderful way to start the day!"

I'm a college student and I've found that hugging is a great way to help relieve the pressures of school. Every morning, many of us greet each other with hugs. What a wonderful way to start the day!

Douglas Smith
Schoolcraft, Michigan

I belong to Overeaters Anonymous and we hug everyone there (or as many as we can) after each meeting. We genuinely care about each other, so that's where all my "hugging experience" comes from. Sometimes I say to my boyfriend, "1-2-3 HUG!" and we both laugh and hug several times.

People don't show affection enough in this insane, mixed up, cold world.

A Hug Lover

(Ed. Note: The following letter was written on the official letterhead of a well-known penitentiary.)

By the way, I'm not the commissioner or the warden of this dump—just another guy with a number. I "borrowed" their grandiose letterhead.

Well, it's about time we recognized one of the truly honest-to-God pleasures in life! A hug is similar to hearing and enjoying the good-sounding smack of a kiss. Boy, they sure don't make 'em like they used to. Of course there is none of the above here, and these guys won't be getting even close.

As mentioned, I'm a number residing in a cell. But the big difference is I'm getting OUT soon. (Pardon the Whoopee!) Also, I'll never return—too old for this nonsense. So maybe I'll be able to spread the "Let's Hug" virtue on as soon as I meet some sensible, decent ladies and gentlemen.

R.J.
New York State

I teach nursery school, and my kids are between 2½ and 3½. Boy, do they like hugs! It's so sad when a child says, "My mom doesn't hug me." When I hugged one little boy he said, "You love me, don't you?" Yes, I love him. What the world needs now is hugs. Real hugs.

Jeanne Bakelar
Sparta, New Jersey

Now that I have become, at least chronologically, an adult, the hugs have become fewer and farther between—and of much lower quality. What passes for a hug now would barely have been an H before. I'm not saying that life before always greeted me with open arms. I've always had a near-fatal deficiency of vitamin H, but now it's worse. So, just as the third-worlder is obsessed with food, I am preoccupied

"What the world needs now is hugs."

with hugs, or a lack thereof.

What is a cynical 21-year-old student like me supposed to do? I want to find out what the rest of this world thinks about hugs, and what they do about it. Goodbye for now, and I'll be waiting to hear from you with open arms. Hug, hug, hug.

Chris Pope
Milton, Delaware

I am a member of Alcoholics Anonymous and we hug all the time. I'm also English and we don't hug in England. Afraid, I guess.

Name Withheld

I'm curious. My life has centered around my children since 1973 when my wife left. I have done everything possible to prove that I love them. My oldest daughter is on her own, providing me with my first grandson—very proud. My next son is all misery—dope, booze, 17 years old going on 100, knows everything. I just can't seem to reach him. Next son no trouble; 16 years old, helps out around the house, seems to understand my sadness. He gave me a *Hug Coupon*. When I was really feeling down he gave me the card and kissed me. It made me feel nine feet tall.

J.E.F.

My huggy friends and I got into hugging when that study came out saying people need a minimum of four hugs per day. When we went our separate ways for the summer we worried that we might not get our minimum daily requirements. So we created our own written symbol (so easy that even a hungover, sleep-deprived college student can do it) to add hugs to our letters, posters, notes, car windshields, dust graffiti, etc. When you can't be with your friends you can still send them your hugs. Long live long-distance hugging—the next best thing to hugging there.

Jeanette Kania
Spotswood, New Jersey

♥

HINT #2 FROM PAUL PLANET

How To Get Relief From The Winter Blahs

If you need fast relief this winter, hugs are there. Whether you're snowed in or battling the winter doldrums, you can depend on hugs. Hugs instantly lift your spirits and speed relief for the winter blahs. No expensive airline tickets required.

Hugs. Pat-pat, squeeze-squeeze... oh what a relief it is.

SUPERB FEELING
AND MORE

© ONCE UPON A PLANET

More affection ● More love
● More relaxation

We're moving hugging into the future. And
we'd like your help. For more fun than ever
before, try hugging.

Paul Planet   School of Life
May 3, 1983   Grade A

Why I Love HUGGING

I love HUGGING because it's beautiful, divine, elevating, enchanting, exhilarating, fun, fundamental, genuine, great, heavenly, important, incredible, joyous, magical, magnificent, mystical, necessary, nifty, outrageous, pleasing, positive, refreshing, relaxing, remarkable, serene, significant, simple, soothing, special, stimulating, stupendous, super, terrific, therapeutic, touching, uncommon, unsurpassed, uplifting, useful, valuable, vital, warm, and worthwhile. That's why I love HUGGING.

Chapter ♥ Nine

Bright Ideas

The Best Things To Do While Hugging:

- Nothing
- Watch a sunrise
- Watch a sunset
- Say, "I really like you!"
- Say, "I love you!"
- Say, "Let's do this more often."
- Feel great.

MAILBAG

Each month I put a message on my phone-answering machine to amuse my callers. Some people leave messages and others call up just to hear the tape. Here's the message I got from you and put on my machine for the month of April:

"Greetings and salutations: Don't wait for someone else to make the first move. Take advantage of your constitutional right to bear arms. Join the new volunteer army: it's exciting, it feels good, it's tax free, gratifying and misunderstood. After all, we are all comrades in arms. Don't put off what you can do today. Bear your arms, GIVE A HUG—it's everlasting. The next move is up to you."

George J. Molteni
Paterson, New Jersey

"...I've lost 25 lbs. on my new hug diet."

Last summer I participated in a Special Olympic event for handicapped children, and we had "huggers" who met the children at the finish line with a great big hug. The kids and the huggers loved it. What a wonderful idea. Love and hugs.

Pearl E. Flynn
South Amboy, New Jersey

Would you believe I've lost 25 lbs. on my new HUG DIET? In only six weeks? I've found some friends who are just hugging the weight right off me! One friend uses the hug coupon I gave him to collect the 1,000,000,000 hugs I promised him, and measures the weight loss at the same time! Now there is less and less of me to hug, but the quality is even better.

When I'm hungry, or scared, or sad or lonely, instead of running to the refrigerator, I run to the arms of a hugging friend. When I'm all hugged up I don't need to eat, and I don't have to feel guilty either!

It's the most fun diet I've ever tried.

Susie Thornley
Mt. Hermon, California

Thanksgiving Day can be exhausting for the cook, especially if she or he gets stuck in the kitchen. So I used *Hug Coupons* as placecards on the dinner table, and I had people traipsing in and out of the kitchen all day getting their hugs and hugging me back. They all laughed, but they were all in there hugging (*and* helping out). I didn't feel a bit tired at the end of the day.

Mrs. Jeanne Rosano
Placerville, California

Members of the Youth Social Department of our local YMCA—about 25 boys and girls between the ages of 10 and 12—provide car washes, bake sales, and other useful community services. When people give us donations for the services, we hand out *Hug Coupons* in return. It's our best idea.

Youth Counselor-YMCA
Houston, Texas

A friend of mine has a real hugging success story. She volunteered to sell hugs for $1 at a local Easter Seal Benefit last week. In a little more than an hour she had made $70! A real hugger's high!

Carolyn Kellams
San Francisco, California

At a recent national conference of College and University Residence Hall Associations there was a competition for spirit. Our school's motto was "SMSU Bears Hug Better." Our 21 delegates went around and hugged almost everyone at the conference, about 1,000 people. Plus we gave out little bears. At the end of the conference there was an awards presentation, and SMSU won the "best spirit" award for hugging.

Susan Holesinger
Ballwin, Missouri

At my 50th birthday party, we gave out *Hug* and *Kiss Coupons* which were a great success and a lot of fun. Everyone wanted to keep their coupons after they were redeemed, I guess for future use.

Naomi Yale
Salt Lake City, Utah

This past Halloween, with the big scare about poisoned medicines and foods, trust in fellow humans spiralled to another low. Many communities cancelled Halloween practices. Our town left the decision up to parents. A small number of children ventured out, under close supervision.

I didn't blame the public caution, but I pitied the younger children who missed the fun of dressing up, surprising friends and neighbors, and, of course, gathering goodies. Despite the dismal mood I decided to try my best to re-instill some trust.

I dressed up in a straw hat, mascara, freckles, and plumped myself with a pillow in my farmer jeans. I pinned a "Participating Human Being" tag on myself. Armed with a batch of *Hug Coupons*, I set forth to visit neighbors, pulling a "trick" by handing them a *Hug Coupon* and a big hug. "Hug Halloween" was a hit everywhere I went—no cavities, no danger of poisoning or tampering; and warm feelings for everyone! The best things in life really are free. Peace to you all.

Lisa Purcell
Lewistown, Pennsylvania

"The best things in life really are free."

My secret's out. People always thought I just loved to give hugs when actually I like *getting* them just as much. I'm the publicity co-ordinator at my church and we sell *Hug Coupons* as a fund-raising project, and just to promote hugging.

Caren Davis
Panama City, Florida

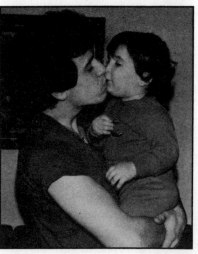

♥

Mini Poster

PHOTOCOPY AND CUT ALONG DOTTED LINE

HEAR YE! HEAR YE!

Let it be known that

_____

is granted full permission to touch, feel, hug, hold, caress, embrace, cuddle, or in any way, shape, or form bestow upon

_____

the gifts of love and/or affection at any time, in any place, for any and/or no reason whatsoever.

The All-New Hug Diet

How It Works

The Hug Diet works on a substitution basis. For fattening foods you substitute something less fattening, something you like just as much. The risk here is that you will grow to like the substitutes better than food, and you may forget to eat at all. All hug dieters should force themselves to eat an adequate amount of vitamins and minerals. The special extras of this meal plan have made it a favorite antidote for the dejection and deprivation and general all-around bad temper that accompany most diets.

Cheating

The ordinary dieter usually reaches the breaking point by the fifth hour of a new diet and goes on an eating binge. This will *never* happen with the *All-New Hug Diet*—because the only way you can cheat is to neglect your daily quota of hugs—and who would do a thing like that? Furthermore, a hug binge will never hurt you. *You Cannot O.H. (over hug) On The Hug Diet!*

Hug-Conversion Chart

The hug-conversion chart gives the number of hugs you need to substitute for some of your favorite foods. *Note:* Different people will have to make slight adjustments in the conversion ratio since hugging is not an exact science.

Food	Equals	Hugs
½ lb. chocolate chip cookies	2 hugs	
½ lb. macaroni salad	1 hug, plus a pat on the back	
Apple pie á la mode	2½ hugs	
Chocolate mousse	14 hugs, and a hug from your cat	
8 potato chips	8 hugs	
150 peanuts	150 hugs	
1 doughnut	12 hugs	
Fried onion rings	1 bear hug, and 4 little doggy hugs	
Cheese cake	5 hugs and 2 pats on the head	
Spaghetti and meatballs	10 hugs and 4 minutes of tickling	
Pepperoni pizza, no anchovies	36 dozen hugs and one hand over your mouth	

Hug Notes

From The Desk Of
A HUGGER

Hug Messages

PHOTOCOPY AND CUT
ALONG DOTTED LINE

WHILE YOU WERE OUT
HUGGING

TO_____

DATE_____ TIME_____

M_____

OF_____

PHONE_____

TELEPHONED		RETURNED YOUR CALL	
PLEASE CALL		NEEDS A HUG	
WILL CALL AGAIN		SO WAS I	

STOPPED IN FOR A HUG	
I WAS WORKING REAL HARD	

MESSAGE_____

_____

_____

_____

_____

© ONCE UPON A PLANET Box 220 Bayside NY 11361

Chapter Ten

I Went to a Fabulous Party!

Invitation

PHOTOCOPY AND CUT ALONG DOTTED LINE

You're Invited to a Hug Party Because:

- ☐ You're the world's greatest hugger
- ☐ It wouldn't be a party without you
- ☐ You'll stay and help clean up
- ☐ You'll add hugs to the party
- ☐ Someday you'll be rich and famous
- ☐ My mother asked me to
- ☐ You're so huggable and cuddly
- ☐ If you hug so will everyone else
- ☐ You're my hug therapist
- ☐ It's at your place
- ☐ You're my main squeeze
- ☐ The all-new Hug Arm-y wants you!
- ☐ I like you
- ☐ We could all use a few more hugs
- ☐ You give great arm
- ☐ _____

Please try to make it.
R.S.V.P.

Calendar Of Reasons

JANUARY   1 New Year's Day 2 Hugover day 3 Oleo margarine patented 4 Consciousness day 5 1st woman governor elected 6 Blizzard of '86 7 Charles Addams's birthday 8 Soupy Sales's birthday 9 Friendship day 10 Jim Croce's birthday 11 Polyester day 12 We're not here forever day 13 Happy day 14 1st "Today Show" 15 Martin Luther King Jr's birthday 16 Nehru Suit goes out of style 17 Mayans discover chocolate 18 Alice falls into rabbit hole 19 Neon sign patented 20 Sun enters Aquarius 21 Telly Savalas's birthday 22 "Who loves ya" day 23 Ernie Kovacs's birthday 24 Eskimo Pie patented 25 1st Social Security check mailed 26 Paul Newman's birthday 27 It's great to be alive day 28 Alan Alda's birthday 29 M.U.S.H. day 30 Wheel invented 31 1st U.S. satellite launched

FEBRUARY   1 X-rays discovered 2 Groundhug day 3 Silly day 4 Candy corn invented 5 Hank Aaron's birthday 6 Babe Ruth's birthday 7 Beatles' 1st U.S. visit 8 Keep in touch day 9 Carole King's birthday 10 1st singing telegram 11 Burt Reynold's birthday 12 Lincoln's Birthday 13 Telephone patented 14 Valentine's Day 15 Valentine's Day II, The Sequel 16 Sonny Bono's birthday 17 "I've Got You Babe" day 18 Sun enters Pisces 19 Phonograph patented 20 1st 3-D movie shown 21 "I Miss You Babe" day 22 Washington's Birthday 23 Cinderella's anniversary 24 1st float parade 25 Zeppo Marx's birthday 26 Jackie Gleason's birthday 27 Peace of Stolbova 28 Yellowstone becomes 1st national park

MARCH   1 Peace Corps starts 2 Dr. Seuss's birthday 3 Who? day 4 Copyright Act passed 5 It's O.K. to be afraid day 6 Lou Costello's birthday 7 Coin locker patented 8 A very special day 9 Mickey Spillane's birthday 10 Harriet Tubman's birthday 11 Blizzard of '88 12 James Taylor's birthday 13 Pluto identified 14 Cotton gin patented 15 Sabu's birthday 16 Jerry Lewis's birthday 17 St. Patrick's Day 18 Feel good day 19 Heh Heh Heh day 20 Sun enters Aries 21 1st day of spring 22 O.K. day 23 Patrick Henry's "Liberty or Death" speech 24 Elton John's birthday 25 Why? day 26 Why not? day 27 Hubba-hubba day 28 Toaster oven discovered 29 Pun day 30 "Seward's Folly" 31 Richard Chamberlain's birthday

APRIL   1 April Fool's Day 2 1st show "As the World Turns" 3 1st Pony Express 4 1st American newspaper 5 Hug a co-worker day 6 Procrastination day 7 1st American camel race 8 Hank Aaron's 715th home run 9 1st free American library 10 Catamaran patented 11 Keep in touch day 12 1st use of catcher's mask 13 Thomas Jefferson's birthday 14 Pan American day 15 1st school for the deaf 16 Pepperoni pizza day 17 Pineapple cheese patented 18 Paul Revere's ride 19 Halley's Comet 20 Sun enters Taurus 21 Planet day 22 Earth day 23 1st motion picture shown 24 Soda fountain invented 25 Nifty day 26 *Citizen Kane* voted best movie ever made 27 Secretaries' Day 28 Keen day 29 Duke Ellington's birthday 30 Louisiana Purchase

MAY   1 Smokey the Bear retires 2 Spiro Agnew disbarred 3 Can day 4 Awareness day 5 1st American in space 6 Willie Mays's birthday 7 Day before Mother's Day day 8 Mother's Day 9 Day after Mother's Day day 10 Fred Astaire's birthday 11 Far out day 12 Just another day day 13 Stay home and hug day 14 The "We want beer" march 15 1st public sale of nylons 16 All the world's a stage day 17 Norwegian independence 18 Ya, shure day 19 1st Jumping Frog Jubilee 20 Lindbergh takes off 21 Sun enters Gemini 22 Laurence Olivier's birthday 23 Grow old along with me day 24 Brooklyn Bridge opens 25 Ruth's last home run 26 Not April Fool's day 27 Golden Gate Bridge opens 28 Piano patented 29 Patrick Henry's birthday 30 Memorial Day 31 Forgetaboutit day

JUNE   1 Reach out day 2 Chow Mein invented 3 "Well I'll be" day 4 Do unto others day 5 Superman's debut 6 1st drive-in movie opens 7 It's been real day 8 Vacuum cleaner invented 9 1st showing of *Cleopatra* 10 Judy Garland's birthday 11 Gene Wilder's birthday 12 Hug someone with a tattoo day 13 Beginning of Father's Week 14 Flag Day 15 Harry Nilsson's birthday 16 Get the "point" day 17 1st woman in space 18 Paul McCartney's birthday 19 Father's Day 20 1st "Ed Sullivan Show" 21 Long-playing record introduced 22 1st day of summer 23 1st balloon flight in America 24 Typewriter patented 25 1st color TV show 26 Bicycle patented 27 Capt. Kangaroo's birthday 28 Mel Brooks's birthday 29 Antoine de St. Exupery's birthday 30 1st show "The Guiding Light"

For A Hug Party

JULY 1 Canada Day 2 1st "Lawrence Welk Show" 3 Quebec founded by Champlain 4 Independence Day 5 P.T. Barnum's birthday 6 Beatrix Potter's birthday 7 Ringo Starr's birthday 8 Silent majority day 9 Vocal minority day 10 1st color motion pictures 11 Goedesic day 12 R. Buckminster Fuller's birthday 13 Cheech's birthday 14 Bastille Day 15 National Ice Cream day 16 Ginger Rogers's birthday 17 Tickle day 18 Honesty day 19 Meek shall inherit the earth day 20 1st man on moon 21 Totally awesome day 22 What's going on? day 23 Sun enters Leo 24 Amelia Earhart's birthday 25 Mother-in-Law's day 26 George Bernard Shaw's birthday 27 Korean War armistice 28 Boat invented 29 Gilroy Garlic festival 30 Casey Stengel's birthday 31 End of July day

AUGUST 1 Shredded wheat patented 2 Who cares? day 3 Hot line installed 4 1st special delivery 5 1st talking movie shown 6 Lucille Ball's birthday 7 Revolving door patented 8 Dustin Hoffman's birthday 9 1st bowling magazine published 10 The Vinny Fotchaboom Doctrine signed 11 Parking meter invented 12 Cantinflas's birthday 13 Bert Lahr's birthday 14 Airline food invented 15 Birds of a feather day 16 Woodstock festival 17 Klondike gold discovery 18 Robert Redford's birthday 19 Orville Wright's birthday 20 Dress like a chicken day 21 Hawaii becomes 50th state 22 Liquid soap patented 23 Sun enters Virgo 24 Allies liberated Paris 25 Orbit day 26 Women's Equality Day 27 Confucius's birthday 28 Think about it day 29 Chop Suey invented 30 Let's dance day 31 All hugs day

SEPTEMBER 1 Emma Nutt becomes 1st telephone operator 2 Geronimo retires 3 1st show "Search for Tomorrow" 4 1st commercial electric lights 5 Labor Day 6 White bread day 7 Do it day 8 Literacy day 9 Expectant Mother's Day 10 1st "Gunsmoke" show 11 Grandparent's Day 12 Dozen day 13 "Star Spangled Banner" written 14 Typewriter ribbon patented 15 Agatha Christie's birthday 16 "Here's looking at you, kid" day 17 Citizenship day 18 1st *N.Y. Times* 19 Look at your feet day 20 Peace day 21 H.G. Wells's birthday 22 Ice cream cone invented 23 Autumnal Equinox 24 1st dirigible flight 25 Phil Rizzuto's birthday 26 Nixon-Kennedy debate 27 1st "Tonight Show" 28 Book matches patented 29 Gotcha day 30 Last day of September day

OCTOBER 1 1st World Series game 2 Groucho Marx's birthday 3 1st "Captain Kangaroo" show 4 Dodgers win their 1st World Series 5 Poet's day 6 1st showing of the *Jazz Singer* 7 1st "American Bandstand" show 8 Take the day off day 9 1st electric blanket sold 10 *Porgy & Bess* opens on Broadway 11 Glass wool patented 12 Columbus Day 13 Paul Simon's birthday 14 Sound barrier broken 15 Sweetest day 16 Squeeze me tight day 17 Health day 18 Meatball discovered 19 Spaghetti day 20 Mickey Mantle's birthday 21 Fabulous day 22 Catherine Deneuve's birthday 23 Sun enters Scorpio 24 United Nations Day 25 1st electronic wristwatch 26 Rocky Marciano becomes champ 27 1st Walt Disney show 28 Statue of Liberty dedicated 29 Richard Dreyfuss's birthday 30 Ballpoint pen patented 31 Halloween

NOVEMBER 1 All Saints' Day 2 Most saints' day 3 Some saints' day 4 No saints' day 5 Guy Fawkes day 6 Electric shaver patented 7 Republican elephant's birthday 8 Bonnie Raitt's birthday 9 Pilgrims reach Cape Cod 10 Snuggle day 11 Veteran's Day 12 Peace of Zsvitva-Torok 13 1st artificial snow for skiing 14 1st street car 15 Potato chip invented 16 Self-hug day 17 Nixon's "I'm not a crook" speech 18 Bagel invented 19 Gettysburg Address 20 Robert Kennedy's birthday 21 Blackout of '65 22 Sun enters Sagittarius 23 Harpo Marx's birthday 24 Boss's day 25 Evaporated milk patented 26 Charles Schulz's birthday 27 Daylight saving time ends 28 1st skywriting demonstration 29 Thanksgiving Day 30 Mark Twain's birthday

DECEMBER 1 Maybe day 2 1st trans-Atlantic telephone wedding 3 Humility day 4 Trash compactor invented 5 Walt Disney's birthday 6 Take five day 7 Harry Chapin's birthday 8 Meander day 9 Roller skates patented 10 1st scented movie shown 11 Boll Weevil monument erected 12 Golf tee patented 13 Chocolate chip invented 14 Nostradamus's birthday 15 Bill of Rights adopted 16 Boston Tea Party 17 Wright brothers' Kitty Hawk flight 18 1st panda arrives in U.S. 19 Corrugated paper patented 20 Score day 21 Frank Zappa's birthday 22 1st day of winter 23 Federal Reserve System started 24 Christmas Eve 25 Christmas Day 26 Coffee percolator patented 27 *Showboat* opens on Broadway 28 Chewing gum patented 29 1st YMCA 30 Bo Diddley's birthday 31 New Year's Eve

Hug Games

The Caterpillar

A sure-fire method to achieve a satisfying group hug.

Everyone stands in a line shoulder to shoulder, facing the same direction. Person 1 turns around and hugs Person 2, then goes on to hug Person 3. When Person 1 gets to Person 4, Person 2 hugs Person 3, and it moves along that way, until the line returns to its original order (or until people get "hugged out"). The Caterpillar works for any number of people and is easy to grasp when demonstrated.

Submitted by Anita Miller Bine, Carrollton, Georgia, who learned the Caterpillar at a Unitarian Church retreat.

Blindperson's Hug

Someone is blindfolded and spun around. The "blindperson" then tries to catch other players who make sounds and duck away. The "blindperson" can call "1, 2, 3, STOP" at any time, and everyone must freeze in position. She/he then feels around for the nearest person and tries to guess who it is. If right, she/he gets a hug and that person becomes the new "blindperson."

Spin The Bottle

The players sit in a circle and someone spins a bottle placed in the center. The player the bottle points to when it comes to rest must hug the person who spun the bottle. She/he then spins the bottle and play continues. If the bottle points to the person who spun it, she/he gets a self-hug, then spins again.

London Bridge

Two people form an arch with hands joined. The other guests pass under the arch singing the verses. When the words "My Fair Lady" are sung, a person gets caught in the "bridge" and gets a sandwich hug.

Hide And Seek

Somebody hides in a safe place when no one is looking. When a signal is given, the players search throughout to find him/her. The first person to discover the hiding place gets a hug.

Fun Raising

If you're thinking about throwing a hug party, consider raising money for your favorite charity at the same time. Hugging is a great theme for any fund raiser, all by itself or as a sideline to a major event (for example, a hug booth at a cake sale, bazaar, or flea market).

Charge admission or request donations. Hugs can be "sold" by the squeeze, raffled, auctioned off or offered as bonuses in conjunction with the purchase of other items. A local or national celebrity would be a natural to improve attendance as well as participation.

Create your own hug coupons or order them through us (see page 126). Sell them for a nickel or a dime or a quarter each and offer to redeem one or all on the spot.

The possibilities are vast. Use imagination. Plan carefully and do it. When it comes to hugging, everyone benefits.

Hug Diploma

PHOTOCOPY AND CUT
ALONG DOTTED LINE

Embraceable University

The Board of Highest Education of the Planet Earth

confers upon

_____

the degree of

Master of the Finest Art in Hugging

together with all the honors, rights, privileges, and hugs pertaining thereto, in recognition of some real good hugging.

_____ Dated _____   _____ Signed _____

Chapter Eleven

Huggers Unite!

Starting a Hug Club

Membership

A hug club can be as small as two people, or as large as the whole world. Sometimes hug clubs function within other, more traditional, clubs. For example, a ski club may have a "hug branch." Churches frequently have hug auxiliaries, as do Overeaters Anonymous.

Age

Any age group can start a hug club; successful clubs often get started with mixed age groups—children and adults.

Rules

There are no rules.

Qualifications

Everyone is qualified.

Getting Members

A little flier describing the history of the club, the purpose, and the activities should be distributed to prospective members. This should be accompanied by an application form.

Application

Name _____

Address _____

Telephone Number _____

Briefly, what do you like best about hugging? _____

_____

Activities

Most hug clubs are started for the sheer pleasure of it. Clubs often extend their activities to benefit others. Some activities that hug clubs have participated in include:

1. Hug sessions for the elderly

2. Patient hug sessions in convalescent hospitals

3. Hug booths at bazaars

4. Distribution of *Hug Coupons* at bake sales and other activities

5. Supplying "Hug Greeters" at conventions

Publicity

The more publicity you have, the more the good word will spread about hugging. Think up activities that attract attention. Send a "Hug Clown" to a party or hospital, sell hugs at a benefit. Newsletters, handbills, posters, bulletin boards, T-shirts, local newspapers, local radio stations and fliers all support the Hug Crusade. Publicity aims for good will, increased membership, and promotion of hugging.

Planning

Consider:

Why—you're starting a club

What—your goals are

How—you can achieve your purpose

Remember to:

- Use the talents of members
- Find a leader with tireless arms
- Include everyone in the plan

Committees

All clubs have committees. At the very least you need a committee to appoint a time and place of the next meeting and to notify other members and prospective members. The next step should be the adoption of a constitution and bylaws. A sample constitution follows.

The Hug Club Constitution

Name of Club _____

Purpose: To celebrate hugging. To encourage this activity wherever we may be; to pledge ourselves to open arms to all human beings, regardless of race, color, creed, size, age, occupation. Remember, dogs and cats and rabbits and all God's creatures need hugs too.

Eligibility: Everyone   **Size of Membership:** Unlimited

Pledge

(Taken with two arms extended)

I pledge my arms to Hugging and promise to do my best to make this planet safe for Hugocracy. Neither shyness nor embarrassment nor fear or rejection shall keep me from my chosen a-rounds.

Hug Club
Membership Card

Name _____

Address _____

City _____ State _____ Zip _____

Signature of Cardholder _____

LIFETIME MEMBER

Hugger's Motto: We're not here forever, so *Let's Hug!* today.

MAILBAG

At our Huggers' Ski Club, Inc., everyone hugs. Yet hugging doesn't seem to be well accepted by people in general. Some think it means an attachment. I feel that hugging is great, a cure for any ill.

Patty Baratta
Rochester, New York

A group from our church is actively promoting encouraging hugs. I have a list of folks that I must hug each Sunday in order to get through the day. I get to practice every day on my wife, but Sunday is really special. Our group is slowly growing as we reach out to others. We missed handing out *Hug Coupons* over the Christmas season, but intend to pass them out during the burnout months of January and February.

"Hugger" Killam
Dallas, Texas

"Our group is slowly growing as we reach out to others."

The Iowa United Methodist Church Conference Council on Youth Ministries (CCYM) set the theme "Hugging Creates Miracles" for their 1982 State Youth Festival.

Duane Philgreen
Independence, Iowa

I started a *"Let's Hug"* in our Methodist Church after listening to one of Dr. Leo Buscaglia's lectures on television. Although there are still a few "touch-me-nots," most everyone responds to the loving gesture. We find that hugging leaves us with a warm, friendly feeling that seems to go with church.

Mary Longhofer
Marion, Kansas

CONTACT Teleministries is a 24-hour-a-day telephone counseling, crisis intervention, and referral ministry. There are over 100 CONTACT centers in the United States, and more centers located in Canada, Australia, Korea, and South Africa. The phones are answered by trained volunteers.

Our 1982 National Conference had as its theme "The Family," meaning individual family units and the CONTACT family as a group. What could be better for families than hugging?

Our local center promoted hugging in our "Hugger Herald" and other promos that we send to the other CONTACT centers throughout the United States. HUGS.

Mary Ann Ramsey
Huntington, West Virginia

"What could be better for families than hugging?"

Hello to you, too. Out here on the West Coast we started Hugs Unlimited about a year ago and we have 1,500 members and are growing fast. We want to get as much Hug News out there as we can. We have a hug newsletter and T-shirts that say, "A Hug a day keeps the grumpies away." Hugs to you and yours.

Myrna Moore
Manhattan Beach, California

♥

By Popular Demand

A special offer for hug lovers. The following prices are available to nonprofit organizations as well as individuals who wish to share these items in any noncommercial way.

Hug Coupons - printed with black and red ink on 2"x3½" card stock.

Pack of 6 cards	.25
Pack of 100 cards	3.00
Box of 500 cards	10.00
Box of 1,000 cards	18.00

Let's Hug! Booklets-the original 32-page 4"x5½" version of the book you are holding.

1-5	1.00 (ea.)
6-10	.75 (ea.)
11-24	.60 (ea.)
25 or more	.50 (ea.)

Hug Licenses - printed in three colors to duplicate the appearance of the New York State driver's license. Complete with lamination.

1-5	.75 (ea.)
6-10	.60 (ea.)
11-24	.50 (ea.)
25 or more	.40 (ea.)

Buttons - "I'm A Participating Human Being" printed white with red background on a 1¾" button.

1-5	.50 (ea.)
6-10	.40 (ea.)
11-24	.35 (ea.)
25 or more	.30 (ea.)

Hug Kits - includes pack of 6 Hug Coupons, license with lamination and an "I'm A Participating Human Being" button.

1-5	1.25 (ea.)
6-10	1.00 (ea.)
11-24	.90 (ea.)
25 or more	.80 (ea.)

Send all orders to:

HUG DESK
Once Upon A Planet
Box 220
Bayside, NY 11361

Minimum Order: five dollars ($5) (does not include shipping)
Shipping: $1.00-UPS or Parcel Post
Terms: Payment with order, check or money order
Sales Tax: New York State residents must include correct sales tax
Foreign Orders: We do not ship outside of the United States
Delivery: Bank checks or money orders - 2 to 4 weeks; personal checks - 4 to 6 weeks
Prices valid thru Dec. 1984

This Isn't The End

Well, we've done everything but stand on our heads to convince you to hug more people more often. But we're not finished. Hugging isn't a fad. *Let's Hug!* isn't just another book to read and shelve. Keep it handy. Use it, share it, refer to it often.

Planet Books is committed to working on new projects to further the cause. Meanwhile, we'd like to hear about your reactions, your thoughts, your feelings, your opinions, your hug experiences. Please write:

HUG MAILBAG
c/o Planet Books
Box 220
Bayside, N.Y. 11361